Owning Up

By Janine Amos and Annabel Spenceley
Consultant Rachael Underwood

CHERRYTREE BOOKS

A Cherrytree book

Designed and produced by
A S Publishing

Published by Cherrytree Press, a division of Evans Publishing Group
2A Portman Mansions
Chiltern St
London W1U 6NR

Reprinted 2006

British Library Cataloguing in Publication Data
Amos, Janine
 Owning Up. - (Growing Up)
  1. Truthfulness and falsehood - Juvenile literature
  2. Conscience - Juvenile literature
  1. Title
  177.3

   ISBN 1 84234 007 7
   ISBN (from 1 Jan 2007) 978 1 84234 007 3

Printed in Malaysia

Emma and Dad

The kitchen's a mess.

Dad cleans it up.

He washes the dishes.
He cleans the floor.

He clears the table.
He throws all the rubbish away.

Emma comes in.
"Where's my model?" she asks.
"It was on the table."

Dad looks at Emma.
He looks at the bin.

"I made a mistake, Emma," says
Dad. "I put your model in the bin.

Emma is upset.
Her dad gives her a hug.

"I'm sorry," says Dad. "That model was important to you, wasn't it?"

Emma nods her head.
How does she feel?

"Why don't we find somewhere safe
to keep your models?" says Dad.
"How about that drawer?"

"Yes!" agrees Emma.
"We'll need to empty it first," Dad
tells her.

Let's do it now!" says Emma.
"OK," says Dad.

Emma makes another model.

And Dad clears up the kitchen.

Ann and Kadeem

"Chug! chug! I'm building a tractor," says Ann.

Ann works hard. The tractor is
finished. She looks in the box for
a driver.

Kadeem comes to build a train.

He picks up Ann's tractor and pulls it apart. He uses the tractor to make his train.

"Hey! Where's my tractor?" Ann asks.
"I used it in my train," says Kadeem.
"I didn't know."

How do you think Ann feels?
How does Kadeem feel?
What could they do?

Kadeem thinks hard.
"You can play with my train," he says.

"But I want a tractor," Ann tells him.

Kadeem thinks again.

"We could make a new tractor,"
he says.

"Yes – with red wheels," agrees Ann.

Together they build a new tractor.

Sometimes people make mistakes.
Some mistakes upset other people.
If you make a mistake like this,
you can own up.

You can tell the other person what
you did. Talk to them. Tell them what
happened. It may help them to
understand. Perhaps you can think
of a way to make things better.